Understanding
PRAYER

Its Purpose, Its Power,
Its Potential

Understanding
PRAYER

Its Purpose, Its Power, Its Potential

E.M. Bounds

BARBOUR
PUBLISHING

© 2013 by Barbour Publishing, Inc.

ISBN 978-1-62029-803-9

eBook Editions:
Adobe Digital Edition (.epub) 978-1-62416-014-1
Kindle and MobiPocket Edition (.prc) 978-1-62416-013-4

Text of this book has been excerpted from the E. M. Bounds books *Purpose in Prayer*, *Power through Prayer*, and *The Weapon of Prayer*. Text has been lightly updated for ease of reading.

All scripture quotations are taken from the King James Version of the Bible.

Published by Barbour Publishing, Inc., P.O. Box 719, Uhrichsville, Ohio 44683, www.barbourbooks.com

Our mission is to publish and distribute inspirational products offering exceptional value and biblical encouragement to the masses.

ecpa Member of the
Evangelical Christian
Publishers Association

Printed in the United States of America.

Contents

1
Ask of Me

My Creed leads me to think that prayer is
efficacious, and surely a day's asking God to
overrule all events for good is not lost. Still there
is a great feeling that when a man is praying
he's doing nothing, and this feeling makes us give
undue importance to work, sometimes even to
the hurrying over or even to the neglect of prayer.
Do not we rest in our day too much on the arm
of flesh? Cannot the same wonders be done now
as of old? Do not the eyes of the Lord run to
and fro throughout the whole earth still to show
Himself strong on behalf of those who put their
trust in Him? Oh that God would give me more
practical faith in Him! Where is now the Lord God
of Elijah? He is waiting for Elijah to call on Him.

JAMES GILMOUR OF MONGOLIA

The more praying there is in the world the better the world will be, the mightier the forces
against evil everywhere. Prayer, in one phase of
its operation, is a disinfectant and a preven-
tive. It purifies the air; it destroys the contagion

of evil. Prayer is no fitful, short-lived thing. It is no voice crying unheard and unheeded in the silence. It is a voice that goes into God's ear, and it lives as long as God's ear is open to holy pleas, as long as God's heart is alive to holy things.

God shapes the world by prayer. Prayers are deathless. The lips that uttered them may be closed in death, the heart that felt them may have ceased to beat, but the prayers live before God, and God's heart is set on them and prayers outlive the lives of those who uttered them: outlive a generation, outlive an age, outlive a world.

That man is the most immortal who has done the most and the best praying. They are God's heroes, God's saints, God's servants, God's representatives. A man can pray better because of the prayers of the past; a man can live holier because of the prayers of the past. The man of many and acceptable prayers has done the truest and greatest service to the incoming generation. The prayers of God's saints strengthen the unborn generation against the desolating waves of sin and evil. Woe to the generation of sons who find their censers empty of the rich incense of prayer; whose fathers have been too busy or too unbelieving to pray, and perils inexpressible and consequences untold are their unhappy heritage. Fortunate are they whose fathers and mothers have left them a wealthy heritage of prayer.

The prayers of God's saints are the capital stock in heaven by which Christ carries on His great work upon earth. The great throes and mighty convulsions on earth are the results of these prayers. Earth is changed, revolutionized, angels move on more powerful, more rapid wings, and God's policy is shaped as the prayers are more numerous, more efficient.

It is true that the mightiest successes that come to God's cause are created and carried on by prayer. God's day of power, the angelic days of activity and power, are when God's Church comes into its mightiest inheritance of mightiest faith and mightiest prayer. God's conquering days are when the saints have given themselves to mightiest prayer. When God's house on earth is a house of prayer, then God's house in heaven is busy and effective in its plans and movements, then His earthly armies are clothed with the triumphs and spoils of victory and His enemies defeated on every hand.

God rests the very life and prosperity of His cause on prayer. This condition was put on the very existence of God's cause in this world. "Ask of Me" is the one condition God puts on the very advance and triumph of His cause.

Men are to pray—to pray for the advance of God's cause. Prayer puts God in full force in the world. To a prayerful man God is present in realized force; to a prayerful Church God is present in glorious power, and the second Psalm is the divine description of the establishment of God's cause through Jesus Christ. All inferior commands have merged in the enthronement of Jesus Christ. God declares the enthronement of His Son. The nations are incensed with bitter hatred against His cause. God is described as laughing at their powerless hate. The Lord will laugh; The Lord will have them in derision. "Yet have I set my king upon my holy hill of Zion" (Psalm 2:6). The decree has passed immutable and eternal:

I will declare the decree:
the LORD hath said unto me,
Thou art My Son;
this day have I begotten thee.
Ask of me, and I shall give thee the
heathen for thine inheritance,
and the uttermost parts of the
earth for thy possession.
Thou shalt break them with a rod of iron;
thou shalt dash them in pieces
like a potter's vessel.
PSALM 2:7–9

"Ask of Me" is the condition for a praying people, willing and obedient. "Prayer also shall be made for him continually" (Psalm 72:15). Under this universal and simple promise men and women of old laid themselves out for God. They prayed and God answered their prayers, and the cause of God was kept alive in the world by the flame of their praying.

Prayer became the settled and only condition to move His Son's kingdom. "Ask, and it shall be given you; seek, and ye shall find; knock, and it shall be opened" (Matthew 7:7).

The strongest one in Christ's kingdom is he who is the best knocker. The secret of success in Christ's Kingdom is the ability to pray. The one who can wield the power of prayer is the strong one, the holy one in Christ's kingdom. The most important lesson we can learn is how to pray.

Prayer is the keynote of the most sanctified life, of the holiest ministry. He does the most for God who is the highest skilled in prayer. Jesus Christ exercised His ministry after this order.

My Response

....

....

....

....

....

....

....

....

....

....

....

....

....

....

My Response

....

....

....

....

....

....

....

....

....

....

....

....

....

....

2
Pray without Ceasing

*That we ought to give ourselves to God
with regard to things both temporal and
spiritual, and seek our satisfaction only in the
fulfilling His will, whether He lead us
by suffering, or by consolation, for all would
be equal to a soul truly resigned. Prayer is
nothing else but a sense of God's presence.*
BROTHER LAWRENCE

*Be sure you look to your secret duty; keep that
up whatever you do. The soul cannot prosper
in the neglect of it. Apostasy generally begins
at the closet door. Be much in secret fellowship
with God. It is secret trading that enriches the
Christian. Pray alone. Let prayer be the key of
the morning and the bolt at night. The best way
to fight against sin is to fight it on our knees.*
PHILIP HENRY

*The prayer of faith is the only power in the
universe to which the Great Jehovah yields.
Prayer is the sovereign remedy.*
ROBERT HALL

An hour of solitude passed in sincere and earnest prayer, or the conflict with and conquest over a single passion or subtle bosom sin will teach us more of thought, will more effectually awaken the faculty and form the habit of reflection than a year's study in the schools without them.

COLERIDGE

A man may pray night and day and deceive himself, but no man can be assured of his sincerity who does not pray. Prayer is faith passing into act. A union of the will and intellect realizing in an intellectual act. It is the whole man that prays. Less than this is wishing or lip work, a sham or a mummery. If God should restore me again to health I have determined to study nothing but the Bible. Literature is inimical to spirituality if it be not kept under with a firm hand.

RICHARD CECIL

Our sanctification does not depend upon changing our works, but in doing that for God's sake which we commonly do for our own. The time of business does not with me differ from the time of prayer. Prayer is nothing else but a sense of the presence of God.

BROTHER LAWRENCE

Let me burn out for God. After all, whatever
God may appoint, prayer is the great thing.
Oh that I may be a man of prayer.

HENRY MARTYN

The possibilities and necessity of prayer, its power and results, are manifested in arresting and changing the purposes of God and in relieving the stroke of His power. Abimelech was smitten by God:

> *So Abraham prayed unto God: and God*
> *healed Abimelech, and his wife, and his*
> *maidservants; and they bare children.*
> *For the LORD had fast closed up all*
> *the wombs of the house of Abimelech,*
> *because of Sarah Abraham's wife.*
> GENESIS 20:17–18

Job's miserable, mistaken comforters had behaved in their controversy with Job so that God's wrath was kindled against them. "My servant Job shall pray for you," said God, "for him will I accept" (Job 42:8).

"And the LORD turned the captivity of Job,

when he prayed for his friends" (Job 42:10).

Jonah was in dire condition when "the LORD sent out a great wind into the sea, and there was a mighty tempest" (Jonah 1:4). When lots were cast, "the lot fell upon Jonah" (Jonah 1:7). He was cast overboard into the sea, but "the LORD had prepared a great fish to swallow up Jonah. . . . Then Jonah prayed unto the LORD his God out of the fish's belly . . . . And the Lord spake unto the fish, and it vomited out Jonah upon the dry land" (Jonah 1:17; 2:1, 10).

When the disobedient prophet lifted up his voice in prayer, God heard and sent deliverance.

"Yet forty days, and Nineveh shall be overthrown" (Jonah 3:4). It was the purpose of God to destroy that great and wicked city. But Nineveh prayed, covered with sackcloth; sitting in ashes she cried "mightily unto God," and "God repented of the evil, that he had said that he would do unto them; and he did it not" (Jonah 3:10).

Pharaoh was a firm believer in the possibilities of prayer, and its ability to relieve. When staggering under the woeful curses of

God, he pleaded with Moses to intercede for him. "Intreat the Lord for me," was his pathetic appeal four times repeated when the plagues were scourging Egypt. Four times were these urgent appeals made to Moses, and four times did prayer lift the dread curse from the hard king and his doomed land.

The blasphemy and idolatry of Israel in making the golden calf and declaring their devotions to it were a fearful crime. The anger of God waxed hot, and He declared that He would destroy the offending people. The Lord was very angry with Aaron also, and to Moses He said, "Let me alone, that I may destroy them" (Deuteronomy 9:14). But Moses prayed, and kept on praying; day and night he prayed for forty days. He made this record of his prayer struggle. "I fell down," he says, "before the LORD, as at the first, forty days and forty nights: I did neither eat bread, nor drink water, because of all your sins which ye sinned, in doing wickedly in the sight of the LORD, to provoke Him to anger. For I was afraid of the anger and hot displeasure, wherewith the LORD was wroth against you to destroy you. But the

LORD hearkened unto me at that time also. And the LORD was very angry with Aaron to have destroyed him: and I prayed for Aaron also the same time" (Deuteronomy 9:18–20).

The message of God to Hezekiah was "Set thine house in order; for thou shalt die, and not live" (2 Kings 20:1). Hezekiah turned his face toward the wall, and prayed to the Lord, and said: "O LORD, remember now how I have walked before thee in truth and with a perfect heart, and have done that which is good in thy sight. And Hezekiah wept sore" (2 Kings 20:3). God said to Isaiah, "Tell Hezekiah. . .I have heard thy prayer, I have seen thy tears. . . . I will add unto thy days fifteen years" (2 Kings 20:5–6).

These men knew how to pray and how to prevail in prayer. Their faith in prayer was no passing attitude that changed with the wind or with their own feelings and circumstances; it was a fact that God heard and answered, that His ear was ever open to the cry of His children, and that the power to do what was asked of Him was equal to His willingness. And thus these men, strong in faith and in prayer, "subdued kingdoms, wrought righteousness, obtained promises, stopped the mouths of lions. Quenched the violence of fire, escaped the edge of the sword, out of weakness were made strong, waxed valiant in fight, turned to flight the armies of the aliens" (Hebrews 11:33–34).

Everything then, as now, was possible to the men and women who knew how to pray. Prayer, indeed, opened a limitless storehouse, and God's hand withheld nothing. Prayer introduced those who practiced it into a world of privilege, and brought the strength and wealth of heaven down to the aid of finite man. What rich and wonderful power was theirs who had learned the secret of victorious approach to God!

And yet, strange as it seems when we contemplate the wonders of which God's people had been witness, there came a slackness in prayer. The mighty hold upon God, that had so often struck awe and terror into the hearts of their enemies, lost its grip. The people, backslidden and unfaithful, had gone off from their praying—if the bulk of them had ever truly prayed. The Pharisee's cold and lifeless praying was substituted for any genuine approach to God, and because of that formal method of praying the whole worship became a parody of its real purpose. A glorious dispensation, and gloriously executed, was it by Moses, by Ezra, by Daniel and Elijah, by Hannah and Samuel; but the circle seems limited and short-lived; the praying ones were few and far between. They had no survivors, none to imitate their devotion to God, none to preserve the roll of the elect.

In vain had the decree established the divine order, the divine call. Ask of Me. From the earnest and fruitful crying to God they turned their faces to pagan gods and cried in vain for the answers that could never come. And so they sank into that godless and pitiful state of those who have lost their purpose in life when the link with the eternal has been broken. Their favored method of prayer was forgotten; they knew not how to pray.

What a contrast to the achievements that brighten up other pages of holy writ. The power working through Elijah and Elisha in answer to prayer reached down even to the very grave. In each case a child was raised from the dead, and the powers of famine were broken. "The effectual fervent prayer of a righteous man availeth much" (James 5:16). Elijah was a man of like passions with us. He prayed fervently that it might not rain, and it rained not on the earth for three years and six months. And he prayed again, and the heaven gave rain, and the earth brought forth her fruit. Jonah prayed while imprisoned in the great fish, and he came to dry land, saved from storm and sea and monsters of the deep by the mighty energy of his praying.

How wide the gracious provision of the grace of praying as administered in that marvelous way. They prayed wondrously. Why could not their praying save the dispensation from decay and death? Was it not because they lost the fire without which all praying degenerates into a lifeless form? It takes effort and toil and care to prepare the incense. Prayer is not work for the lazy. When all the rich, spiced graces from the body of prayer have by labor and beating been blended and refined and intermixed, the fire is needed to unloose the incense and make its fragrance rise to the throne of God. The fire that consumes creates the spirit and life of the incense. Without fire prayer has no spirit; it is, like dead spices, for corruption and worms.

The casual, intermittent prayer is never bathed in this divine fire. For the man who thus prays is lacking in the earnestness that lays hold of God, determined not to let Him go until the blessing comes. "Pray without ceasing" (1 Thessalonians 5:17), counseled the great apostle. That is the habit that drives prayer right into the mortar that holds the building stones together. "You can do more than pray after you have prayed," said the godly Dr. A. J. Gordon, "but you cannot do more than pray until you have prayed." The story of every great Christian achievement is the history of answered prayer.

"The greatest and the best talent that God gives to any man or woman in this world is the talent of prayer," writes Principal Alexander Whyte. "And the best usury that any man or woman brings back to God when He comes to reckon with them at the end of this world is a life of prayer. And those servants best put their Lord's money 'to the exchangers' who rise early and sit late, as long as they are in this world, ever finding out and ever following after better and better methods of prayer, and ever forming more secret, more steadfast, and more spiritually fruitful habits of prayer, till they literally 'pray without ceasing,' and till they continually strike out into new enterprises in prayer, and new achievements, and new enrichments."

Martin Luther, when once asked what his plans, for the following day were, answered: "Work, work, from early until late. In fact, I have so much to do that I shall spend the first three hours in prayer." Cromwell, too, believed in being much upon his knees. Looking on one occasion at the statues of famous men, he turned to a friend and said: "Make mine kneeling, for thus I came to glory."

It is only when the whole heart is gripped with the passion of prayer that the life-giving fire descends, for none but the earnest man gets access to the ear of God.

My Response

....

....

....

....

....

....

....

....

....

....

....

....

....

....

My Response

....

....

....

....

....

....

....

....

....

....

....

....

....

....

My Response

....

....

....

....

....

....

....

....

....

....

....

....

....

....

3
The Purpose of All Real Prayer

Lord Jesus, cause me to know in my daily experience the glory and sweetness of Thy name, and then teach me how to use it in my prayer, so that I may be even like Israel, a prince prevailing with God. Thy name is my passport, and secures me access; Thy name is my plea, and secures me answer; Thy name is my honor and secures me glory. Blessed Name, Thou art honey in my mouth, music in my ear, heaven in my heart, and all in all to my being!

C. H. Spurgeon

I do not mean that every prayer we offer is answered exactly as we desire it to be. Were this the case, it would mean that we would be dictating to God, and prayer would degenerate into a mere system of begging. Just as an earthly father knows what is best for his children's welfare, so does God take into consideration the particular needs of His human family, and meets them out of His wonderful storehouse. If our

petitions are in accordance with His will, and if
we seek His glory in the asking, the answers will
come in ways that will astonish us and fill our
hearts with songs of thanksgiving. God is a rich
and bountiful Father, and He does not forget
His children, nor withhold from them anything
which it would be to their advantage to receive.

J. KENNEDY MACLEAN

The example of our Lord in the matter of prayer is one that His followers might well copy. Christ prayed much, and He taught much about prayer. His life and His works, as well as His teaching, are illustrations of the nature and necessity of prayer. He lived and labored to answer prayer. But the necessity of persistence in prayer was the emphasized point in His teaching about prayer. He taught not only that we must pray, but that we must persevere in prayer.

He taught in command and precept the idea of energy and earnestness in praying. He gives to our efforts graduation and climax. We are to ask, but to the asking we must add seeking, and seeking must pass into the full force of our effort in knocking. The pleading soul must be aroused to effort by God's silence. Denial, instead of preventing or disconcerting, must arouse its latent energies and kindle anew its highest zeal.

In the Sermon on the Mount, in which Jesus lays down the cardinal duties of His religion, He not only gives prominence to prayer in general and secret prayer in particular, but He sets apart a distinct and different section to give weight to persistent prayer. To prevent any discouragement in praying He lays as a basic principle the fact of God's great fatherly willingness—that God's willingness to answer our prayers exceeds our willingness to give good and necessary things to our children, just as far as God's ability, goodness, and perfection exceed our infirmities and evil. As a further assurance and stimulant to prayer, Christ gives the most positive and repeated assurance of answer to prayers. He declares: "Ask, and it shall be given you; seek, and ye shall find; knock, and it shall be opened unto you" (Matthew 7:7). And to make our assurance doubly sure, He adds: "For every one that asketh receiveth; and he that seeketh findeth; and to him that knocketh it shall be opened" (Matthew 7:8).

Why does He unfold to us the Father's loving readiness to answer the prayers of His children? Why does He affirm so strongly that prayer will be answered? Why does He repeat that positive affirmation six times? Why does Christ on two distinct occasions go over the same strong promises, iterations, and reiterations in regard to the certainty of prayer being answered? Because He knew that there would be many delayed answers, which would call for persistent pressing, and that if our faith did not have the strongest assurance of God's willingness to answer, delay would break it down. And that our spiritual laziness would come in, under the guise of submission, and say it is not God's will to give what we ask, and so we would cease praying and lose our case. After Christ had put God's willingness to answer prayer in a very clear and strong light, He then urges us to diligence, and that every unanswered prayer, instead of decreasing our pressure should only increase intensity and energy. If asking does not get, let asking pass into the settled attitude and spirit of seeking. If seeking does not secure the answer, let seeking pass on to the more energetic and clamorous plea of knocking. We must persevere till we get it. There is no failure here if our faith does not break down.

As our great example in prayer, our Lord puts love as a primary condition—a love that has purified the heart from all the elements of hate, revenge, and ill will. Love is the supreme condition of prayer, a life inspired by love. First Corinthians 13 is the law of prayer as well as the law of love. The law of love is the law of prayer, and to master this chapter from the epistle of Saint Paul is to learn the first and fullest condition of prayer.

Christ taught us also to approach the Father in His name. That is our passport. It is in His name that we are to make our petitions known. "Verily, verily, I say unto you, He that believeth on me, the works that I do shall he do also; and greater works than these shall he do; because I go unto my Father. And whatsoever ye shall ask in my name, that will I do, that the Father may be glorified in the Son. If ye shall ask any thing in my name, I will do it" (John 14:12–14).

How wide and comprehensive is that "whatsoever." There is no limit to the power of that name. "Whatsoever ye shall ask"—that is the divine declaration, and it opens up to every praying child a vista of infinite resource and possibility.

And that is our heritage. All that Christ has may become ours if we obey the conditions. The one secret is prayer. The place of revealing and of equipping, of grace and of power, is the prayer chamber, and as we meet there with God we shall not only win our triumphs but we shall also grow in the likeness of our Lord and become His living witnesses to men.

Without prayer the Christian life, robbed of its sweetness and its beauty, becomes cold and formal and dead; but rooted in the secret place where God meets and walks and talks with His own, it grows into such a testimony of divine power that all people will feel its influence and be touched by the warmth of its love. Thus, resembling our Lord and Master, we shall be used for the glory of God and the salvation of all people.

And that, surely, is the purpose of all real prayer and the end of all true service.

My Response

....

....

....

....

....

....

....

....

....

....

....

....

....

My Response

....

....

....

....

....

....

....

....

....

....

....

....

....

My Response

....

....

....

....

....

....

....

....

....

....

....

....

....

....

4
People of Prayer Needed

Study universal holiness of life. Your whole usefulness depends on this, for your sermons last but an hour or two; your life preaches all the week. If Satan can only make a covetous minister a lover of praise, of pleasure, of good eating, he has ruined your ministry. Give yourself to prayer, and get your texts, your thoughts, your words from God. Luther spent his best three hours in prayer.

ROBERT MURRAY McCHEYNE

We are constantly on a stretch, if not on a strain, to devise new methods, new plans, new organizations to advance the church and secure enlargement and efficiency for the Gospel. This trend of the day has a tendency to lose sight of the man or sink the man in the plan or organization. God's plan is to make much of the man, far more of him than of anything else.

[Editor's note: Bounds wrote the following chapter specifically to preachers—but his message of the necessity of prayer in the Christian's witness to the world applies to all of us.]

Men are God's method. The church is looking for better methods; God is looking for better men. "There was a man sent from God, whose name was John" (John 1:6). The process that heralded and prepared the way for Christ was bound up in that man John. "Unto us a child is born, unto us a son is given" (Isaiah 9:6). The world's salvation comes out of that cradled Son. When Paul appeals to the personal character of the men who rooted the Gospel in the world, he solves the mystery of their success. The glory and efficiency of the Gospel are staked on the men who proclaim it. When God declares that "the eyes of the LORD run to and fro throughout the whole earth, to shew himself strong in the behalf of them whose heart is perfect toward him" (2 Chronicles 16:9), he declares the necessity of men and his dependence on them as a channel through which to exert his power upon the world. This vital, urgent truth is one that this age of machinery is apt to forget. Forgetting it is as damaging to the work of God as would be the striking of the sun from the sky. Darkness, confusion, and death would ensue.

What the church needs today is not more

machinery or better, not new organizations or more and novel methods, but men whom the Holy Ghost can use—men of prayer, men mighty in prayer. The Holy Ghost does not flow through methods, but through men. He does not come on machinery, but on men. He does not anoint plans, but men—men of prayer.

A well-known historian has said that the accidents of personal character have more to do with the revolutions of nations than either philosophic historians or democratic politicians will allow. This truth applies in full to the Gospel of Christ, the character and conduct of the followers of Christ—who Christianize the world, transfigure nations and individuals. Of the preachers of the Gospel it is eminently true.

The character as well as the fortunes of the Gospel are committed to the preacher. He makes or mars the message from God to man. The preacher is the golden pipe through which the divine oil flows. The pipe must not only be golden, but open and flawless, that the oil may have a full, unhindered, unwasted flow.

The man makes the preacher. God must

make the man. The messenger is, if possible, more than the message. The preacher is more than the sermon. The preacher makes the sermon. As the life-giving milk from the mother's bosom is the mother's life, so all the preacher says is colored, impregnated by what the preacher is. The treasure is in earthen vessels, and the taste of the vessel impregnates and may discolor. The man, the whole man, lies behind the sermon. Preaching is not the performance of an hour. It is the outflow of a life. It takes twenty years to make a sermon, because it takes twenty years to make the man. The true sermon is a thing of life. The sermon grows because the man grows. The sermon is forceful because the man is forceful. The sermon is holy because the man is holy. The sermon is full of the divine fervor because the man is full of the divine fervor.

Paul termed it "my gospel;" not that he had degraded it by his personal eccentricities or diverted it by selfish appropriation, but the Gospel was put into the heart and lifeblood of the man Paul, as a personal trust to be executed by his Pauline traits, to be set aflame and empowered by the fiery energy of his fiery soul. Paul's sermons—what were they? Where are they? Skeletons, scattered fragments, afloat on the sea of inspiration! But the man Paul, greater than his sermons, lives forever, in full form, feature, and stature, with his molding hand on the church. The preaching is but a voice. The voice in silence dies, the text is forgotten, the sermon fades from memory; the preacher lives.

The sermon cannot rise in its life-giving forces above the man. Dead men give out dead sermons, and dead sermons kill. Everything depends on the spiritual character of the preacher. The Jewish high priest had inscribed in jeweled letters on a golden frontlet: "Holiness to the Lord." So every preacher in Christ's ministry must be molded into and mastered by this same holy motto. It is a crying shame for the Christian ministry to fall lower in holiness of character and holiness of aim than the Jewish priesthood. Jonathan Edwards said: "I went on with my eager pursuit after more holiness and conformity to Christ. The heaven I desired was a heaven of holiness." The Gospel of Christ does not move by popular waves. It has no self-propagating power. It moves as the men who have charge of it move. The preacher must impersonate the Gospel. Its divine, most distinctive features must be embodied in him. The constraining power of love must be in the preacher as a projecting, eccentric, all-commanding, self-oblivious force. The energy of self-denial must be his being, his heart and blood and bones. He must go forth as a man among men, clothed with humility, abiding in meekness, wise as a serpent, harmless as a dove; the bonds of a servant with the spirit of a king, a king in high, royal, dependent bearing, with the simplicity and sweetness of a child. The preacher must throw himself, with all the abandon of a perfect, self-emptying faith and a self-consuming zeal, into his work for the salvation of men. Hearty, heroic, compassionate, fearless martyrs must the men be who take hold of and shape a generation for God. If they be timid time servers; place seekers; if they be men pleasers or men fearers; if their faith has a weak hold on God or His Word; if their denial be broken by any phase of self or the world, they cannot take hold of the church nor the world for God.

The preacher's sharpest and strongest preaching should be to himself. His most difficult, delicate, laborious, and thorough work must be with himself. The training of the twelve was the great, difficult, and enduring work of Christ. Preachers are not sermon makers, but men makers and saint makers, and only he who has made himself a man and a saint is well-trained for this business. It is not great talents nor great learning nor great preachers that God needs, but men great in holiness, great in faith, great in love, great in fidelity, great for God— men always preaching by holy sermons in the pulpit, by holy lives out of it. These can mold a generation for God.

After this order, the early Christians were formed. Men they were of solid mold, preachers after the heavenly type—heroic, stalwart, soldierly, saintly. Preaching with them meant self-denying, self-crucifying, serious, toilsome, martyr business. They applied themselves to it in a way that told on their generation, and formed in its womb a generation yet unborn for God. The preaching man is to be the praying man. Prayer is the preacher's mightiest weapon. An almighty force in itself, it gives life and force to all.

The real sermon is made in the closet. The man—God's man—is made in the closet. His life and his most profound convictions were born in his secret communion with God. The burdened and tearful agony of his spirit, his weightiest and sweetest messages were gotten when alone with God. Prayer makes the man; prayer makes the preacher; prayer makes the pastor.

The pulpit of this day is weak in praying. The pride of learning is against the dependent humility of prayer. Prayer is too often with the pulpit only officially—a performance for the routine of service. Prayer is not to the modern pulpit the mighty force it was in Paul's life or Paul's ministry. Every preacher who does not make prayer a mighty factor in his own life and ministry is weak as a factor in God's work and is powerless to project God's cause in this world.

My Response

....

....

....

....

....

....

....

....

....

....

....

....

....

....

My Response

....

....

....

....

....

....

....

....

....

....

....

....

....

5
Great Prayers and Pray-ers

*The potency of prayer hath subdued the strength
of fire; it had bridled the rage of lions, hushed
the anarchy to rest, extinguished wars, appeased
the elements, expelled demons, burst the chains
of death, expanded the gates of heaven, assuaged
diseases, repelled frauds, rescued cities from
destruction, stayed the sun in its course, and
arrested the progress of the thunderbolt. Prayer is
an all-efficient panoply, a treasure undiminished,
a mine which is never exhausted, a sky
unobscured by clouds, a heaven unruffled by
the storm. It is the root, the fountain, the
mother of a thousand blessings.*

CHRYSOSTOM

*The prayers of holy men appease God's wrath,
drive away temptations, resist and overcome the
devil, procure the ministry and service of angels,
rescind the decrees of God. Prayer cures sickness
and obtains pardon; it arrests the sun in its
course and stays the wheels of the chariot of the
moon; it rules over all gods and opens and shuts
the storehouses of rain, it unlocks the cabinet*

of the womb and quenches the violence of fire;
it stops the mouths of lions and reconciles our
suffering and weak faculties with the violence of
torment and violence of persecution; it pleases
God and supplies all our need.

JEREMY TAYLOR

More things are wrought by prayer
Than this world dreams of.
Wherefore, let thy voice
Rise like a fountain for me night and day.
For what are men better than sheep or goats,
That nourish a blind life within the brain,
If, knowing God, they lift not hands of prayer
Both for themselves and those who call them friend?
For so the whole round earth is every way
Bound by gold chains about the feet of God.

TENNYSON

Perfect prayer is only another name for love.

FENELON

It was said of the late C. H. Spurgeon, that he glided from laughter to prayer with the naturalness of one who lived in both elements. With him the habit of prayer was free and unfettered. His life was not divided into compartments, the one shut off from the other with a rigid exclusiveness that barred all intercommunication. He lived in constant fellowship with his Father in heaven. He was ever in touch with God, and thus it was as natural for him to pray as it was for him to breathe.

"What a fine time we have had; let us thank God for it," he said to a friend on one occasion when, out under the blue sky and wrapped in glorious sunshine, they had enjoyed a holiday with the unfettered enthusiasm of schoolboys. Prayer sprang as spontaneously to his lips as did ordinary speech, and never was there the slightest incongruity in his approach to the divine throne straight from any scene in which he might be taking part.

That is the attitude with regard to prayer that ought to mark every child of God. There are, and there ought to be, stated seasons of communication with God when, everything else shut out, we come into His presence to talk to Him and to let Him speak to us; and out of such seasons springs that beautiful habit of prayer that weaves a golden bond between earth and heaven. Without such stated seasons the habit of prayer can never be formed; without them there is no nourishment for the spiritual life. By means of them the soul is lifted into a new atmosphere—the atmosphere of the heavenly city, in which it is easy to open the heart to God and to speak with Him as friend speaks with friend.

Thus, in every circumstance of life, prayer is the most natural outpouring of the soul, the unhindered turning to God for communion and direction. Whether in sorrow or in joy, in defeat or in victory, in health or in weakness, in calamity or in success, the heart leaps to meet with God just as children run to their mother's arms, ever sure that with her is the sympathy that meets every need.

Dr. Adam Clarke, in his autobiography, records that when Mr. Wesley was returning to England by ship, considerable delay was caused by contrary winds. Wesley was reading, when he became aware of some confusion onboard, and asking what was the matter, he was informed that the wind was contrary. "Then," was his reply, "let us go to prayer."

After Dr. Clarke had prayed, Wesley broke

out into fervent supplication which seemed to be more the offering of faith than of mere desire. "Almighty and everlasting God," he prayed. "Thou hast sway everywhere, and all things serve the purpose of Thy will, Thou holdest the winds in Thy fists and sittest upon the water floods, and reignest a King forever. Command these winds and these waves that they obey Thee, and take us speedily and safely to the haven whither we would go."

The power of this petition was felt by all. Wesley rose from his knees, made no remark, but took up his book and continued reading. Dr. Clarke went on deck, and to his surprise found the vessel under sail, standing on her right course. Nor did she change till she was safely at anchor. On the sudden and favorable change of wind, Wesley made no remark; so fully did he expect to be heard that he took it for granted that he was heard.

That was prayer with a purpose—the definite and direct utterance of one who knew that he had the ear of God, and that God had the willingness as well as the power to grant the petition which he asked of Him.

Major D. W. Whittle, in an introduction to the wonders of prayer, says of George Muller, of Bristol: "I met Mr. Muller in the express, the morning of our sailing from Quebec to Liverpool. About half an hour before the tender was to take the passengers to the ship, he asked of the agent if a deck chair had arrived for him from New York. He was answered, 'No,' and told that it could not possibly come in time for the steamer. I had with me a chair I had just purchased, and told Mr. Muller of the place nearby, and suggested, as but a few moments remained, that he had better buy one at once. His reply was, 'No, my brother. Our heavenly Father will send the chair from New York. It is one used by Mrs. Muller. I wrote ten days ago to a brother, who promised to see it forwarded here last week. He has not been prompt, as I would have desired, but I am sure our heavenly Father will send the chair. Mrs. Muller is very sick on the sea, and has particularly desired to have this same chair, and not finding it here yesterday, we have made special prayer that our heavenly Father would be pleased to provide it for us, and we will trust Him to do so.' As this dear man of God went peacefully onboard, running the risk of Mrs. Muller making the trip without a chair, when for a couple of dollars she could have been provided for, I confess I feared Mr. Muller was carrying his faith principles too far and not acting wisely. I was kept at the express office ten minutes after Mr. Muller left. Just as I started to hurry to the wharf, a team drove up the street, and on top of a load just arrived front New York was Mr. Muller's chair. It was sent at once to the tender and placed in my hands to take to Mr. Muller, just as the boat was leaving the dock (the Lord having a lesson for me). Mr. Muller took it with the happy, pleased expression of a child who has just received a kindness deeply appreciated, and reverently removing his hat, and folding his hands over it, he thanked the heavenly Father for sending the chair."

One of Melancthon's correspondences tells of Luther's praying: "I cannot enough admire the extraordinary cheerfulness, constancy, faith, and hope of the man in these trying and vexatious times. He constantly feeds these gracious affections by a very diligent study of the Word of God. Then not a day passes in which he does not employ in prayer at least three of his very best hours. Once I happened to hear him at prayer. Gracious God! What spirit and what faith is there in his expressions! He petitions God with as much reverence as if he was in the divine presence, and yet with as firm a hope and confidence as he would address a father or a friend. 'I know,' said he, 'Thou art our Father and our God; and therefore I am sure Thou wilt bring to naught the persecutors of Thy children. For shouldest Thou fail to do this Thine own cause, being connected with ours, would be endangered. It is entirely Thine own concern. We, by Thy providence, have been compelled to take a part. Thou therefore wilt be our defence.' Whilst I was listening to Luther praying in this manner, at a distance, my soul seemed on fire within me, to hear the man address God so like a friend, yet with so much gravity and reverence; and also to hear him, in the course of his prayer, insisting on the promises contained in the Psalms, as if he were sure his petitions would be granted."

The following is related by a sergeant major

about William Bramwell, a noted Methodist preacher in England, wonderful for his zeal and prayer. "In July, 1811, our regiment was ordered for Spain, then the seat of a protracted and sanguinary war. My mind was painfully exercised with the thoughts of leaving my dear wife and four helpless children in a strange country, unprotected and unprovided for. Mr. Bramwell felt a lively interest in our situation, and his sympathizing spirit seemed to drink in all the agonized feelings of my tender wife. He supplicated the throne of grace day and night in our behalf. My wife and I spent the evening previous to our march at a friend's house, in company with Mr. Bramwell, who sat in a very pensive mood, and appeared to be in a spiritual struggle all the time. After supper, he suddenly pulled his hand out of his bosom, laid it on my knee, and said: 'Brother Riley, mark what I am about to say! You are not to go to Spain. Remember what I tell you, you are not; for I have been wrestling with God on your behalf, and when my heavenly Father condescends in mercy to bless me with power to lay hold on Himself, I do not easily let Him go; no, not until I am favored with an answer. Therefore you may depend upon it that the next time I hear from you, you will be settled in quarters.' This came to pass exactly as he said. The next day the order for going to Spain was countermanded."

These men prayed with a purpose. To them God was not far away in some inaccessible region, but near at hand, ever ready to listen to the call of His children. There was no barrier between. They were on terms of perfect intimacy, if one may use such a phrase in relation to man and his Maker. No cloud obscured the face of the Father from His trusting child, who could look up into the divine countenance and pour out the longings of his heart. And that is the type of prayer that God never fails to hear. He knows that it comes from a heart at one with His own; from one who is entirely yielded to the heavenly plan, and so He bends His ear and gives to the pleading child the assurance that his petition has been heard and answered.

Have we not all had some such experience when with set and undeviating purpose we have approached the face of our Father? In an agony of soul we have sought refuge from the oppression of the world in the anteroom of heaven; the waves of despair seemed to threaten destruction, and as no way of escape was visible anywhere, we fell back, like the disciples of old, upon the power of our Lord, crying to Him to save us lest we perish. And then in the twinkling of an eye, the thing was done. The billows sank into a calm; the howling wind died down at the divine command; the agony of the soul passed into a restful peace as over the whole being there crept the consciousness of the divine presence, bringing with it the assurance of answered prayer and sweet deliverance.

"I tell the Lord my troubles and difficulties, and wait for Him to give me the answers to them," says one man of God. "And it is wonderful how a matter that looked very dark will in prayer become clear as crystal by the help of God's Spirit. I think Christians fail so often to get answers to their prayers because they do not wait long enough on God. They just drop down and say a few words, and then jump up and forget it and expect God to answer them. Such praying always reminds me of the small boy ringing his neighbor's doorbell, and then running away as fast as he can go."

When we acquire the habit of prayer we enter into a new atmosphere. "Do you expect to go to heaven?" asked someone of a devout Scotsman. "Why, man, I live there," was the quaint and unexpected reply. It was a pithy statement of great truth, for the whole journey to heaven is heaven begun to the Christian who walks near enough to God to hear the secrets He has to impart.

This attitude is beautifully illustrated in a story about Horace Bushnell, told by Dr. Parkes Cadman. Bushnell was found to be suffering from an incurable disease. One evening the Rev. Joseph Twichell visited him, and as they sat together under the starry sky, Bushnell said: "One of us ought to pray." Twichell asked Bushnell to do so, and Bushnell began his prayer; burying his face in the earth, he poured out his heart until, said Twichell in recalling the incident, "I was afraid to stretch out my hand in the darkness lest I should touch God."

To have God this near is to enter the holy of holies—to breathe the fragrance of the heavenly air, to walk in Eden's delightful gardens. Nothing but prayer can bring God and man into this happy communion. That was the experience of Samuel Rutherford, just as it is the experience of everyone who passes through the same gateway. When this saint of God was confined in jail at one time for conscience's sake, he enjoyed in a rare degree this divine companionship, recording in his diary that Jesus entered his cell, and that at His coming "every stone flashed like a ruby."

Many others have borne witness to the same sweet fellowship, when prayer had become the one habit of life that meant more than anything else to them. David Livingstone lived in the realm of prayer and knew its gracious influence. It was his habit every birthday to write a prayer, and on his next to last birthday, this was his prayer: "O Divine one, I have not loved Thee earnestly, deeply, sincerely enough. Grant, I pray Thee, that before this year is ended I may have finished my task." It was just on the threshold of the year that followed that his faithful men, as they looked into the hut in Ilala, while the rain dripped from the eaves, saw their master on his knees beside his bed in an attitude of prayer. He had died on his knees in prayer.

Stonewall Jackson was a man of prayer. Said he: "I have so fixed the habit in my mind that I never raise a glass of water to my lips without asking God's blessing, never seal a letter without putting a word of prayer under the seal, never take a letter from the post without a brief sending of my thoughts heavenward, never change my classes in the lecture room without a minute's petition for the cadets who go out and for those who come in."

James Gilmour, the pioneer missionary to Mongolia, was a man of prayer. He had a habit in his writing of never using a blotter. He made a rule when he got to the bottom of any page to wait until the ink dried and spend the time in prayer.

In this way their whole being was saturated with the divine, and they became the reflection of the heavenly fragrance and glory. Walking with God down the avenues of prayer we acquire something of His likeness, and unconsciously we become witnesses to others of His beauty and His grace. Professor James, in his famous work *Varieties of Religious Experience*, tells of a man of forty-nine who said: "God is more real to me than any thought or thing or person. I feel His presence positively, and the more as I live in closer harmony with His laws as written in my body and mind. I feel Him in the sunshine or rain; and all mingled with a delicious restfulness most nearly describes my feelings. I talk to Him as to a companion in prayer and praise, and our communion is delightful. He answers me again and again, often in words so clearly spoken that it seems my outer ear must have carried the tone, but generally in strong mental impressions. Usually a text of scripture, unfolding some new view of Him and His love for me, and care for my safety. . . . That He is mine and I am His never leaves me; it is an abiding joy. Without it life would be a blank, a desert, a shoreless, trackless waste."

Equally notable is the testimony of Sir Thomas Browne, the beloved physician who lived at Norwich in 1605, and was the author of a very remarkable book of wide circulation, *Religio Medici*. In spite of the fact that England was passing through a period of national convulsion and political excitement, he found comfort and strength in prayer. "I have resolved," he wrote in a journal found among his private papers after his death, "to pray more and pray always, to pray in all places where quietness inviteth, in the house, on the highway, and on the street; and to know no street or passage in this city that may not witness that I have not forgotten God." And he adds: "I purpose to take occasion of praying upon the sight of any church which I may pass, that God may be worshipped there in spirit, and that souls may be saved there; to pray daily for my sick patients and for the patients of other physicians; at my entrance into any home to say, 'May the peace of God abide here'; after hearing a sermon, to pray for a blessing on God's truth, and upon the messenger; upon the sight of a beautiful person to bless God for His creatures, to pray for the beauty of such an one's soul, that God may enrich her with inward graces, and that the outward and inward may correspond; upon the sight of a deformed person, to pray God to give them wholeness of soul, and by and by to give them the beauty of the resurrection."

What an illustration of the praying spirit! Such an attitude represents prayer without ceasing, reveals the habit of prayer in its unceasing supplication, in its uninterrupted communion, in its constant intercession. What an illustration, too, of purpose in prayer! Of how many of us can it be said that as we pass people in the street we pray for them, or that as we enter a home or a church we remember the household or the congregation in prayer to God?

The explanation of our thoughtlessness or forgetfulness lies in the fact that prayer with so many of us is simply a form of selfishness; it means asking for something for ourselves— that and nothing more.

And from such an attitude we need to pray to be delivered.

My Response

....

....

....

....

....

....

....

....

....

....

....

....

....

....

My Response

....

....

....

....

....

....

....

....

....

....

....

....

....

....

My Response

....

....

....

....

....

....

....

....

....

....

....

....

....

....

6
Examples of Praying Men

The act of praying is the very highest energy
of which the human mind is capable; praying,
that is, with the total concentration of the
faculties. The great mass of worldly men and of
learned men are absolutely incapable of prayer.

SAMUEL TAYLOR COLERIDGE

Bishop Wilson says: "In H. Martyn's journal the spirit of prayer, the time he devoted to the duty, and his fervor in it are the first things which strike me."

Payson wore the hardwood boards into grooves where his knees pressed so often and so long. His biographer says: "His continuing instant in prayer, be his circumstances what they might, is the most noticeable fact in his history, and points out the duty of all who would rival his eminency. To his ardent and persevering prayers must no doubt be ascribed in a great measure his distinguished and almost uninterrupted success."

The Marquis DeRenty, to whom Christ was most precious, ordered his servant to call him from his devotions at the end of half an hour. The servant at the time saw his face through an aperture. It was marked with such holiness that he hated to arouse him. His lips were moving, but he was perfectly silent. He waited until three half hours had passed; then he called to him. When he arose from his knees he said that the half hour was so short when he was communing with Christ.

Brainerd said: "I love to be alone in my cottage, where I can spend much time in prayer."

William Bramwell is famous in Methodist annals for personal holiness and for his wonderful success in preaching and for the marvelous answers to his prayers. For hours at a time he would pray. He almost lived on his knees. He went over his circuits like a flame of fire. The fire was kindled by the time he spent in prayer. He often spent as many as four hours at a time in prayer.

Bishop Andrewes spent the greatest part of five hours every day in prayer and devotion.

Sir Henry Havelock always spent the first

two hours of each day alone with God. If the encampment was struck at six a.m., he would rise at four.

Earl Cairns rose daily at six o'clock to secure an hour and a half for the study of the Bible and for prayer, before conducting family worship at a quarter to eight.

Dr. Judson's success in prayer can be attributed to the fact that he gave much time to prayer. He says on this point: "Arrange thy affairs, if possible, so that thou canst leisurely devote two or three hours every day not merely to devotional exercises but to the very act of secret prayer and communion with God. Endeavor seven times a day to withdraw from business and company and lift up thy soul to God in private retirement. Begin the day by rising after midnight and devoting some time amid the silence and darkness of the night to this sacred work. Let the hour of opening dawn find thee at the same work. Let the hours of nine, twelve, three, six, and nine at night witness the same. Be resolute in this cause. Make all feasible sacrifices to maintain it. Consider that thy time is short, and that business and company must not be allowed to rob thee of thy God." Impossible, say we, fanatical directions! Dr. Judson impressed an empire for Christ and laid the foundations of God's kingdom with imperishable granite in the heart of Burma. He was successful, one of the few men who mightily impressed the world for Christ. Many men of greater gifts and genius and learning than he have made no such impression; their religious work is like footsteps in the sands, but he has engraved his work on the adamant. The secret of its depth and endurance is found in the fact that he gave time to prayer. He kept the iron red-hot with prayer, and God's skill fashioned it with enduring power. No man can do a great and enduring work for God who is not a man of prayer, and no man can be a man of prayer who does not give much time to praying.

Is it true that prayer is simply the compliance with habit, dull and mechanical? A petty performance into which we are trained until tameness, shortness, and superficiality are its chief elements? "Is it true that prayer is, as is assumed, little else than the half-passive play of sentiment, which flows languidly on through the minutes or hours of easy reverie?" Canon Liddon continues: "Let those who have really prayed give the answer. They sometimes describe prayer with the patriarch Jacob as a wrestling together with an unseen power, which may last, not infrequently in an earnest life, late into the night hours, or even to the break of day. Sometimes they refer to common intercession with St. Paul as a concerted struggle. They have, when praying, their eyes fixed on the Great Intercessor in Gethsemane, upon the drops of blood which fall to the ground in that agony of resignation and sacrifice. Importunity is of the essence of successful prayer. Importunity means not dreaminess but sustained work. It is through prayer especially that the kingdom of heaven suffereth violence, and the violent take it by force. It was a saying of the late Bishop Hamilton that 'No man is likely to do much good in prayer who does not begin by looking upon it in the light of a work to be prepared for and persevered in with all the earnestness which we bring to bear upon subjects which are in our opinion at once most interesting and most necessary.'"

My Response

....

....

....

....

....

....

....

....

....

....

....

....

....

....

My Response

....

....

....

....

....

....

....

....

....

....

....

....

....

....

7
Prayerless Christians

If there was ever a time when Peter, James,
and John needed to remain awake it was in
Gethsemane. If James had persisted in keeping
awake it might have saved his decapitation a
few years later. If Peter had stirred himself to
really intercede for himself and others he would
not have denied his Christ that night in
the palace of Caiaphas.

H. W. HODGE

There is great need in this day for Christian businessmen to infuse their mundane affairs with the spirit of prayer. There is a great army of successful merchants of almost every kind who are members of Christ's Church, and it is high time these men attended to this matter. This is but another version of the phrase "putting God into business," the realization and restraint of His presence and of His fear in all aspects of life. We need the atmosphere of the prayer closet to pervade our public salesrooms and countinghouses. The sanctity of prayer should fill our business. We need the spirit of Sunday carried over to Monday and continued until Saturday. But this cannot be done by prayerless men, but by men of prayer. We need businessmen to go about their concerns with the same reverence and responsibility with which they enter the closet. Men are badly needed who are devoid of greed, but who, with all their hearts carry God with them into the secular affairs of life.

Men of the world imagine prayer to be too ineffective to come into rivalry with business methods and worldly practices. Against such a misleading doctrine Paul sets all the commands of God, the loyalty to Jesus Christ, the claims of godly character, and the demands of the salvation of the world. Men must pray, and put strength and heart into their praying. This is part of the primary business of life, and to it God has called men, first of all.

Praying men are God's agents on earth, the representatives of the government of heaven, set to a specific task on the earth. While it is true that the Holy Spirit and the angels of

God are agents of God in carrying forward the redemption of the human race, yet among them there must be praying men. For such men God has great use. He can make much of them, and in the past has done wonderful things through them. These are His instruments in carrying out God's great purposes on the earth. They are God's messengers, His watchmen, shepherds, workmen, who need not be ashamed. Fully equipped for the great work to which they are appointed, they honor God and bless the world.

Above all things, Christian men and women must, primarily, be leaders in prayer. No matter how involved they may be in other activities, they fail if they are not examples in prayer. They must give their brains and hearts to prayer. Men who make and shape the program of Christ's Church, who map out its line of activity, should themselves be shaped and made by prayer. Men controlling the church finances, thought, and action—should all be men of prayer.

The progress toward the completion of God's work in this world has two basic principles—God's ability to give and man's ability to ask. Failure in either one is fatal to the success of God's work on earth. God's inability to do or to give would put an end to redemption. Man's failure to pray would, just as surely, set a limit to the plan. But God's ability to do and to give has never failed and cannot fail; but man's ability to ask can fail, and often does. Therefore the slow progress that is being made toward the realization of a world won for Christ lies entirely with man's limited asking. There is need for the entire Church of God, on the earth, to commit itself to prayer. The Church upon its knees would bring heaven upon the earth.

The wonderful ability of God to do for us is thus expressed by Paul in one of his most comprehensive statements, "And God is able to make all grace abound toward you," he says, "that ye, always having all sufficiency in all things, may abound to every good work" (2 Corinthians 9:8).

Study, I pray you, that remarkable statement—"God is able to make all grace abound." That is, He is able to give such sufficiency, that we may abound—overflow—to every good work. Why are we not more fully fashioned after this overflowing order? The answer is lack of prayer ability. "Ye have not, because ye ask not" (James 4:2). We are feeble, weak, and impoverished because of our failure to pray. God is restrained in doing because we are restrained by reason of our nonpraying. All failures in securing heaven are traceable to lack of prayer or misdirected petition.

Prayer must be broad in its scope—it must plead for others. Intercession for others is the hallmark of all true prayer. When prayer is confined to self and to the sphere of one's personal needs, it dies by reason of its littleness, narrowness, and selfishness. Prayer must be broad and unselfish or it will perish. Prayer is the soul of a man stirred to plead with God for others. In addition to being interested in the eternal interests of one's own soul it must, in its very nature, be concerned for the spiritual and eternal welfare of others. One's ability to pray for self is greatest when it expresses compassion for others.

In 1 Timothy 2, the apostle Paul urges

with singular and specific emphasis, that those who occupy positions of influence and places of authority, are to give themselves to prayer. "I will therefore that men pray every where" (1 Timothy 2:8). This is the high calling of the men of the church, and no calling is so engaging, so engrossing, and so valuable that we can afford to relieve Christian men from the all-important vocation of secret prayer. Nothing whatever can take the place of prayer. Nothing whatever can atone for the neglect of praying. This is uppermost, first in point of importance and first in point of time. No man is so high in position, or in grace, to be exempt from an obligation to pray. No man is too big to pray, no matter who he is, nor what office he fills. The king on his throne is as much obligated to pray as the peasant in his cottage. None is so high and exalted in this world or so lowly and obscure as to be excused from praying. The help of everyone is needed in completing the work of God, and the prayer of each praying man helps to expand the church. The leaders in place, in gifts, and in authority are to be chiefs in prayer.

Civil and church rulers shape the affairs of this world. And so civil and church rulers themselves need to be shaped personally in spirit, heart, and conduct, in truth and righteousness, by the prayers of God's people. This is in direct line with Paul's words:

> *"I exhort therefore," he says, "that,*
> *first of all, supplications, prayers,*
> *intercessions, and giving of thanks,*
> *be made for all men; for kings,*
> *and for all that are in authority."*
> 1 TIMOTHY 2:1–2

It is a sad day for righteousness when church politics, instead of holy praying, shapes the administration of the kingdom and elevates men to position and power. Why pray for all people? Because God wills the salvation of all people. God's children on earth must link their prayers to God's will. Prayer is to carry out the will of God. God wills the salvation of all people. His heart is set on this one thing. Our prayers must be the creation and advocates of God's will. We are to grasp humanity in our praying as God grasps humanity in His love, His interest, and His plans to redeem humanity. Our sympathies, prayers, wrestling, and ardent desires must run parallel with the will of God—broad, generous, worldwide, and godlike. The Christian must in all things, first of all, be conformed to the will of God, but nowhere shall this royal devotion be more evident than in the salvation of humankind. This high partnership with God, as His representatives on earth, is to have its fullest, richest, and most efficient application in prayer for all people.

Men are to pray for all men, especially for rulers in church and state, "that we may lead a quiet and peaceable life in all godliness and honesty" (1 Timothy 2:2). Peace on the outside and peace on the inside. Praying calms disturbing forces, allays tormenting fears, brings conflict to an end. Prayer tends to do away with turmoil. But even if there are external conflicts, it is well to have deep peace within the citadel of the soul. "That we may lead a quiet and peaceable life." Prayer brings the inner calm and furnishes the outward tranquility. Praying rulers and praying subjects, were they worldwide, would allay turbulent forces, make wars to cease, and peace to reign.

Men must pray for all men that we may lead lives "in all godliness and honesty." That is with godliness and gravity. godliness is to be like God. It is to be godly, to have godlikeness, having the image of God stamped upon the inner nature, and showing the same likeness in conduct and in disposition. Almighty God is the very highest model, and to be like Him is to possess the highest character. Prayer molds us into the image of God, and at the same time tends to mold others into the same image in proportion to our prayers for others. Prayer means to be godlike, and to be godlike is to love Christ and love God, to be one with the Father and the Son in spirit, character, and conduct. Prayer means to stay with God until you are like Him. Prayer makes a godly man, and puts within him "the mind of Christ" (1 Corinthians 2:16), the mind of humility, of self-surrender, of service, of pity, and of prayer. If we really pray, we will become more like God, or else we will quit praying.

"Men pray every where" (1 Timothy 2:8), in the closet, in the prayer meeting, about the family altar, and to do it, "lifting up holy hands, without wrath and doubting" (1 Timothy 2:8). Here is not only the obligation laid upon the men to pray, but instructions as to how they should pray. Men must pray "without wrath." That is, without bitterness against their neighbors or brethren; without the stubbornness and tenacity of a strong will, and hard feelings; without an evil desire or emotion kindled by nature's fires in the sinful nature. Praying is not to be done by these questionable things, nor in company with such evil feelings, but "without" them, aloof and entirely separate from them. This is the sort of praying the men are called upon to do, the sort that God hears and the kind that prevails with God and accomplishes things. With such praying in the hands of Christian men, they become divine agencies in God's hands for carrying on God's gracious purposes and executing His designs in redemption.

Prayer has a higher origin than man's nature. This is true whether we mean man's nature as separate from the angelic nature, or man's sinful nature unrenewed and unchanged. Prayer does not originate in the realms of the carnal mind. Such a nature is entirely foreign to prayer simply because "the carnal mind is enmity against God" (Romans 8:7). It is by the new Spirit that we pray, the new spirit sweetened by the sugar of heaven perfumed with the fragrance of the upper world, and invigorated by a breath from the crystal sea. The "new spirit" is native to the skies, panting after the heavenly things, inspired by the breath of God. It is the praying attitude from which all the old juices of the carnal, unreformed nature have been expelled, and the fire of God has created the flame that has consumed worldly lusts, and the juices of the Spirit have been injected into the soul, and the praying is entirely separate from wrath.

Men are also to pray "without doubting." The Revised Version puts it, "without disputings." Faith in God, belief in God's Word, they must have "without question." No doubting or disputing must be in the mind. There must be no opinions, nor hesitancy, no questioning, no reasoning, no intellectual quibbling, no rebellion, but a strict, steadfast loyalty of spirit to God, a life of loyalty in heart and intellect to God's Word.

God has much to do with believers who have a living, transforming faith in Jesus Christ. These are God's children. A father loves his children, supplies their needs, hears their cries and answers their requests. Children believe their fathers, love them, trust in them, and ask them for what they need, believing without doubting that their fathers will hear their requests. God has everything to do with answering the prayer of His children. Their troubles concern Him, and their prayers awaken Him. Their voices are sweet to Him. He loves to hear them pray, and He is never happier than to answer their prayers.

Prayer is intended for God's ear. It is not man, but God who hears and answers prayer. Prayer covers the whole range of our needs. Hence, "in every thing by prayer and supplication. . .let your requests be made known unto God" (Philippians 4:6). Prayer includes the entire range of God's ability. "Is any thing too hard for the LORD?" (Genesis

18:14). Prayer belongs to no favored segment of our needs, but reaches to and embraces the entire circle of our wants, simply because God is the God of the whole person. God has pledged Himself to supply the needs of the whole person, physical, intellectual, and spiritual. "But my God shall supply all your need according to his riches in glory by Christ Jesus" (Philippians 4:19). Prayer is the child of grace, and grace is for the whole person, and for every one of the children of men.

My Response

....

....

....

....

....

....

....

....

....

....

....

....

....

....

My Response

....

....

....

....

....

....

....

....

....

....

....

....

....

My Response

....

....

....

....

....

....

....

....

....

....

....

....

....

....

8
Much Time Should Be Given to Prayer

The great masters and teachers in Christian doctrine have always found in prayer their highest source of illumination. Not to go beyond the limits of the English Church, it is recorded of Bishop Andrews that he spent five hours daily on his knees. The greatest practical resolves that have enriched and beautified human life in Christian times have been arrived at in prayer.

CANON LIDDON

While many private prayers, in the nature of things, must be short; while public prayers, as a rule, ought to be short and condensed; while there is ample room for and value put on brief prayer—yet in our private communions with God time is a feature essential to its value.

Much time spent with God is the secret of all successful praying. Prayer that is felt as a mighty force is the product of much time spent with God. Our short prayers owe their point and efficiency to the long ones that have preceded them. The short prevailing prayer cannot be prayed by one who has not prevailed with God in a mightier struggle of long continuance. Jacob's victory of faith could not have been gained without that all-night wrestling. God's acquaintance is not made by short visits. God does not bestow His gifts on the casual or hasty comers and goers. Much time alone with God is the secret of knowing Him and of influence with Him. He yields to the persistence of a faith that knows Him. He bestows His richest gifts upon those who declare their desire for and appreciation of those gifts by the constancy as well as earnestness of their persistence. Christ, who in this as well as other things is our example, spent many whole nights in prayer. His custom was to pray much. He had his habitual place to pray. Many long seasons of praying make up his history and character. Paul prayed day and night. It took time from very important interests for Daniel to pray three times a day. David's morning, noon, and night praying were doubtless on many occasions very protracted. While we have no specific account of the time these Bible saints spent in prayer, the indications are that they consumed much time in prayer, and on some occasions long seasons of praying were their custom.

We would not have anyone think that the value of their prayers is to be measured by the clock, but our purpose is to impress on our minds the necessity of being much alone with God; and that if this feature has not been produced by our faith, then our faith is of a feeble and shallow type.

The men who have most fully illustrated Christ in their characters, and have most powerfully affected the world for Him, have been men who spent so much time with God as to make it a notable feature of their lives. Charles Simeon devoted the hours from four to eight in the morning to God. Mr. Wesley spent two hours daily in prayer. He began at four in the morning. Of him, one who knew him well wrote: "He thought prayer to be more his business than anything else, and I have seen him come out of his closet with a serenity of face next to shining." John Fletcher stained the walls of his room by the breath of his prayers. Sometimes he would pray all night: always, frequently, and with great earnestness. His whole life was a life of prayer. "I would not rise from my seat," he said, "without lifting my heart to God." His greeting to a friend was always: "Do I meet you praying?" Luther said: "If I fail to spend two hours in prayer each morning, the devil gets the victory through the day. I have so much business I cannot get on without spending three hours daily in prayer." He had a motto: "He that has prayed well has studied well."

Archbishop Leighton was so often alone with God that he seemed to be in a perpetual meditation. "Prayer and praise were his business and his pleasure," says his biographer. Bishop Ken was so much with God that his soul was said to be God-enamored. He was with God before the clock struck three every morning. Bishop Asbury said: "I propose to rise at four o'clock as often as I can and spend two hours in prayer and meditation." Samuel Rutherford, the fragrance of whose piety is still rich, rose at three in the morning to meet God in prayer. Joseph Alleine arose at four o'clock for his business of praying until eight. If he heard other tradesmen plying their business before he was up, he would exclaim: "O how this shames me! Doth not my Master deserve more than theirs?" He who has learned this trade well withdraws at will, on sight, and with acceptance from heaven's unfailing bank.

One of the holiest and among the most gifted of Scotch preachers says: "I ought to spend the best hours in communion with God. It is my noblest and most fruitful employment, and is not to be thrust into a corner. The morning hours, from six to eight, are the most uninterrupted and should be thus employed. After tea is my best hour, and that should be solemnly dedicated to God. I ought not to give up the good old habit of prayer before going to bed; but guard must be kept against sleep. When I awake in the night, I ought to rise and pray. A little time after breakfast might be given to intercession." This was the praying plan of Robert McCheyne.

John Welch, the holy and wonderful

Scotch preacher, thought the day ill spent if he did not spend eight or ten hours in prayer. He kept a plaid that he might wrap around himself when he arose to pray at night. His wife would complain when she found him lying on the ground weeping. He would reply: "O woman, I have the souls of three thousand to answer for, and I know not how it is with many of them!"

My Response

....

....

....

....

....

....

....

....

....

....

....

....

....

My Response

....

....

....

....

....

....

....

....

....

....

....

....

9
Begin the Day with Prayer

*I ought to pray before seeing anyone. Often when
I sleep long, or meet with others early, it is eleven
or twelve o'clock before I begin secret prayer. This
is a wretched system. It is unscriptural. Christ
arose before day and went into a solitary place.
David says: "Early will I seek thee"; "Thou
shalt early hear my voice." Family prayer loses
much of its power and sweetness, and I can do
no good to those who come to seek from me. The
conscience feels guilty, the soul unfed, the lamp
not trimmed. Then when in secret prayer the soul
is often out of tune, I feel it is far better to begin
with God— to see His face first, to get my soul
near Him before it is near another.*

ROBERT MURRAY McCHEYNE

The men who have done the most for God in
this world have been early on their knees.
He who fritters away the early morning, its
opportunity and freshness, in other pursuits
than seeking God will make poor headway
seeking Him the rest of the day. If God is not

first in our thoughts and efforts in the morning, He will be in the last place the remainder of the day.

Behind this early rising and early praying is the ardent desire that presses us into this pursuit after God. Morning listlessness is the index to a listless heart. The heart that is slow in seeking God in the morning has lost its relish for God. David's heart was passionate after God. He hungered and thirsted after God, and so he sought God early, before daylight. The bed and sleep could not chain his soul in its eagerness after God. Christ longed for communion with God; and so, rising a great while before day, He would go out into the mountain to pray. The disciples, when fully awake and ashamed of their indulgence, would know where to find Him. We might go through the list of men who have mightily impressed the world for God, and we would find them early after God.

A desire for God that cannot break the chains of sleep is a weak thing and will do but little good for God after it has indulged itself fully. The desire for God that falls so far behind the devil and the world at the beginning of the day will never catch up.

It is not simply the getting up that puts men to the front and makes them captain generals in God's hosts, but it is the ardent desire that stirs and breaks all self-indulgent chains. But the getting up gives expression, increase, and strength to the desire. If they had lain in bed and indulged themselves, the desire would have been quenched. The desire aroused them and put them on the stretch for God, and this heeding and acting on the call gave their faith its grasp on God and gave to their hearts the sweetest and fullest revelation of God. And this strength of faith and fullness of revelation made them saints, and the halo of their sainthood has come down to us, and we have enjoyed their conquests. But we take our fill in enjoyment, and not in labor. We build their tombs and write their epitaphs, but are careful not to follow their examples.

We need a generation of preachers who seek God and seek Him early, who give the freshness and dew of effort to God, and secure in return the freshness and fullness of His power that He may be as the dew to them, full of gladness and strength through all the heat and labor of the day. Our laziness after God is our crying sin. The children of this world are far wiser than we. They are at it early and late. We do not seek God with passion and diligence. No man gets God who does not follow hard after Him, and no soul follows hard after God who is not after Him in the early morning.

My Response

....

....

....

....

....

....

....

....

....

....

....

....

....

....

My Response

....

....

....

....

....

....

....

....

....

....

....

....

....

10
Prayer Essential to God

Then shalt thou call, and the LORD shall answer;
thou shalt cry, and he shall say, Here I am. . . .
Then shalt thou delight thyself in the LORD; and I
will cause thee to ride upon the high places of the
earth, and feed thee with the heritage of Jacob thy
father: for the mouth of the LORD hath spoken it.

ISAIAH 58:9, 14

It must never be forgotten that almighty God rules this world. He is not an absentee God. His hand is ever on the throttle of human affairs. He is everywhere present in the concerns of time. "His eyes behold, his eyelids try, the children of men" (Psalm 11:4). He rules the world just as He rules the Church by prayer. This lesson needs to be emphasized, iterated, and reiterated in the ears of men of modern times and brought to bear with cumulative force on the consciences of this generation whose eyes have no vision for the eternal things, whose ears are deaf toward God.

Nothing is more important to God than prayer in dealing with humankind. But it is likewise all-important to man to pray. Failure to pray is failure along the whole line of life. It is failure of duty, service, and spiritual progress. God must help man by prayer. He who does not pray, therefore, robs himself of God's help and places God where He cannot help man. Man must pray to God if love for God is to exist. Faith and hope, and patience and all the strong, beautiful, vital forces of godliness are withered and dead in a prayerless life. The life of the individual believer, his personal salvation, and personal Christian graces have their being, bloom, and fruit in prayer.

All this and much more can be said as to the necessity of prayer to the being and culture of piety in the individual. But prayer has a larger sphere, a more obligated duty, a loftier inspiration. Prayer concerns God, whose purposes and plans are conditioned on prayer. His will and His glory are bound up in praying. The days of God's splendor and renown have always been the great days of prayer. God's great movements in this world have been conditioned on, continued, and fashioned by prayer. God has put Himself in these great movements just as men have prayed. Present, prevailing, conspicuous, and masterful prayer has always brought God to be present. The real and obvious test of a genuine work of God is the prevalence of the spirit of prayer. God's mightiest forces permeate a movement when prayer's mightiest forces are there.

God's movement to bring Israel from Egyptian bondage had its inception in prayer. Thus early did God and the human race put prayer as one of the granite forces upon which His world movements were to be based.

Hannah's petition for a son began a great prayer movement for God in Israel. Praying women, whose prayers like those of Hannah, can give to the cause of God men like Samuel, do more for the Church and the world than all the politicians on earth. Men born of prayer are the saviors of the state, and men saturated with prayer give life and momentum to the Church. Under God they are saviors and helpers of both church and state.

We must believe that the divine record about prayer and God are given that we might be constantly reminded of Him, and be ever refreshed by the faith that God holds His Church for the entire world, and that God's purpose will be fulfilled. His plans concerning the Church will most assuredly and inevitably be carried out. That record of God has been given without doubt that we may be deeply impressed that the prayers of God's saints are a great factor, a supreme factor, in carrying forward God's work, with ease and in time. When the Church is in prayer, God's cause always flourishes and His kingdom on earth always triumphs. When the Church fails to pray, God's cause decays and evil of every kind prevails. In other words, God works through the prayers of His people, and when they fail Him at this point, decline and deadness follow. It is according to the divine plans that spiritual prosperity comes through the prayer channel. Praying saints are God's agents for carrying on His saving and providential work on earth. If His agents fail Him, neglecting to pray, then His work fails. Praying agents of the Most High are always forerunners of spiritual prosperity.

The men of the Church of all ages who have held the Church for God have had in affluent fullness and richness the ministry of prayer. The rulers of the church whom the scriptures reveal had superiority in prayer. They may have been outstanding in culture, in intellect, and in all the natural or human forces; or they may have been lowly in physical achievements and native gifts; yet in each case prayer was the all-potent force in the leadership of the church. And this was so because God was with and in what they did, for prayer always carries us back to God. It recognizes God and brings God into the world to work and save and bless. The most efficient agents in spreading the knowledge of God, in completing His work upon the earth, and in standing as a breakwater against the billows of evil, have been praying church leaders. God depends upon them, employs them, and blesses them.

Prayer cannot be retired as a secondary force in this world. To do so is to retire God from the movement. It is to make God secondary. The prayer ministry is an all-engaging force. It must be so, to be a force at all. Prayer is the sense of God's need and the call for God's help to supply that need. The value and place of prayer is the value and place of God. To give prayer the secondary place is to make God secondary in life's affairs. To substitute other forces for prayer, retires God and materializes the whole movement.

Prayer is an absolute necessity to the proper carrying on of God's work. God has made it so. This must have been the principal reason why in the early Church, when the complaint that the widows of certain believers had been neglected in the daily administration of the church's charity, that the twelve called the disciples together, and told them to look out for seven men, "full of the Holy Ghost and wisdom" (Acts 6:3), whom they would appoint over that benevolent work, adding this important statement, "But we will give ourselves continually to prayer, and to the ministry of the word" (Acts 6:4). They surely realized that the success of the Word and the progress of the Church were dependent in an important sense upon their "giving themselves to prayer." God could effectively work through them in proportion as they gave themselves fully to prayer.

The apostles were as dependent upon prayer as other folks. Sacred work—church activities—may so engage and absorb us as to hinder praying, and when this is the case, evil results always follow. It is better to let the work go by default than to let the praying go by neglect. Whatever affects the intensity of our praying affects the value of our work. "Too busy to pray" is not only the keynote to backsliding, but it mars even the work done. Nothing is well done without prayer for the simple reason that it leaves God out of the account. It is so easy to be seduced by the good to the neglect of the best, until both the good and the best perish. How easily may men, even leaders in Zion, be led by the insidious wiles of Satan to cut short our praying in the interests of the work! How easy to neglect prayer or cut short our praying simply by the plea that we have church work on our hands. Satan has effectively disarmed us when he can keep us too busy doing things to stop and pray.

"Give ourselves continually to prayer, and

to the ministry of the word" (Acts 6:4). The Revised Version has it, "We will continue steadfastly in prayer." The implication of the word *steadfast* used here means "to be strong, steadfast, to be devoted to, to keep at it with constant care, to make a business out of it." We find the same word in Colossians 4:12 and in Romans 12:12, which is translated, "continuing instant in prayer."

The apostles were under the law of prayer, which recognizes God as God and depends upon Him to do for them what He would not do without prayer. They were under the necessity of prayer, just as all believers are, in every age and in every region of the world. They had to be devoted to prayer in order to make their ministry of the Word efficient. The business of preaching is worth very little without it being in direct partnership with the business of praying. Apostolic preaching cannot be carried on unless there is apostolic praying. Alas, that this plain truth has been so easily forgotten by those who minister in holy things! Without in any way passing a criticism on the ministry, we feel it to be high time that somebody or other declared to its members that effective preaching is conditioned on effective praying. The preaching that is most successful is the ministry that has much prayer in it. Perhaps one might go so far as to say that it is the only kind that is successful. God can mightily use the preacher who prays. He is God's chosen messenger for good, whom the Holy Spirit delights to honor, God's efficient agent in saving men and in edifying the saints.

In Acts 6:1–8 we have the record of how, long ago, the apostles felt that they were losing—had lost—in apostolic power because they did not have relief from certain duties in order that they might give themselves more to prayer. So they called a halt because they discovered to their regret that they were too deficient in praying. Doubtless they kept up the form of praying, but it was seriously defective in intensity and in length. Their minds were too much preoccupied with the finances of the church. Just as in this day we find in many places both laymen and ministers are so busily engaged in "serving tables," that they are glaringly deficient in praying. In fact in present-day church affairs men are looked upon as religious because they give largely of their money to the church, and men are chosen for official positions not because they are men of prayer, but because they have the financial ability to run church finances and to get money for the church.

Now these apostles, when they looked into this matter, determined to put aside these hindrances growing out of church finances, and resolved to "give themselves to prayer." Not that these finances were to be ignored or set aside, but ordinary laymen, "full of faith and of the Holy Ghost" (Acts 6:5) could be found, really religious men, who could easily attend to this money business without in the least affecting their devotion or their praying, thus giving them something to do in the church, and at the same time taking the burden from the apostles who would be able now to pray more, and praying more, to be blessed themselves in soul, and at the same time to more effectually do the work to which they had been called.

They realized, too, as they had not realized before, that they were being so pressed by attention to material things, things right in themselves, that they could not give to prayer that strength, ardor, and time that its nature and importance demanded. And so we will discover, under close scrutiny of ourselves sometimes that things legitimate, things right in themselves, things commendable may so en gross our attention, so preoccupy our minds and so draw on our feelings, that prayer may be omitted, or at least very little time may be given to prayer. How easy to slip away from the closet! Even the apostles had to guard themselves at that point. How much do we need to watch ourselves at the same place! Things legitimate and right may become wrong when they take the place of prayer. Things right in themselves may become wrong things when they are allowed to clutter our hearts. It is not only the sinful things that hurt prayer. It is not only questionable things that are to be guarded against. But it is things that are right in their places, but that are allowed to sidetrack prayer and shut the closet door, often with the self-comforting plea that "we are too busy to pray."

Possibly this has had as much to do with

the breaking down of family prayer in this age as any other one cause. It is at this point that family religion has decayed, and just here is one cause of the decline of the prayer meeting. Men and women are too busy with legitimate things to "give themselves to prayer." Other things are given the right of way. Prayer is set aside or made secondary. Business comes first. And this means not always that prayer is second, but that prayer is put entirely out. The apostles drove directly at this point, and determined that even church business should not affect their praying habits. Prayer must come first. Then would they be in deed and truth God's real agents in His world, through whom He could effectually work, because they were praying men, and thereby put themselves directly in line with His plans and purposes, which was that He works through praying men.

When the complaint came to their ears the apostles discovered that what they had been doing did not fully serve the divine ends of peace, gratitude, and unity; but discontent, complaining, and division were the result of their work, which had far too little prayer in it. And so prayer was put prominently to the front.

Praying men are a necessity in carrying out the divine plan for the salvation of men. God has made it so. He established prayer as a divine ordinance, and this implies men are to do the praying. So that praying men are a necessity in the world. The fact that so often God has employed men of prayer to accomplish His ends clearly proves the intention. It is altogether unnecessary to name all the instances where God used the prayers of righteous men to carry out His gracious designs. Time and space are too limited for the list. Yet one or two cases might be named. In the case of the golden calf, when God intended to destroy the Israelites because of their great sin of idolatry when Moses was receiving the law at God's hands, the very existence of Israel was in danger, for Aaron had been swept away by the strong popular tide of unbelief and sin. All seemed lost but Moses and prayer, and prayer became more efficient and wonder-working on behalf of Israel than Aaron's magic rod. God was determined on the destruction of Israel and Aaron. His anger waxed hot. It was a fearful and a critical hour. But prayer was the levee that held back heaven's desolating fury. God's hand was held fast by the interceding of Moses, the mighty intercessor.

Moses was set on delivering Israel. It was with him a long and exhaustive struggle of praying for forty days and forty nights. Not for one moment did he relax his hold on God. Not for one moment did he quit his place at the feet of God, even for food. Not for one moment did he moderate his demand or ease his cry. Israel's existence was in the balance. Almighty God's wrath must be stayed. Israel must be saved at all hazards. And Israel was saved. Moses would not let God alone. And so, today, we can look back and give the credit of the present race of the Jews to the praying of Moses centuries ago.

Persevering prayer always wins; God yields to persistence and fidelity. He has no heart to say no to such praying as Moses did. Actually God's purpose to destroy Israel was changed by the praying of this man of God. It is but an illustration of how much just one person praying is worth in this world, and how much depends upon him.

When Daniel, in Babylon, refused to obey the decree of the king not to ask any petition of any god or man for thirty days, he shut his eyes to the decree that would shut him off from his praying room, and refused to be deterred from calling upon God from fear of the consequences. So he "kneeled upon his knees three times a day" (Daniel 6:10), and prayed as he had before done, leaving it all with God as to the consequences of thus disobeying the king.

There was nothing impersonal about Daniel's praying. It always had an objective, and was an appeal to a great God, who could do all things. There was no coddling of self, nor looking after subjective or reflex influences. In the face of the dreadful decree that would remove him from place and power into the lion's den, "he kneeled upon his knees three times a day, and prayed, and gave thanks before his God, as he did aforetime" (Daniel 6:10). The gracious result was that prayer laid its hands upon an Almighty arm, which intervened in that den of vicious, cruel lions and closed their mouths and preserved His servant Daniel, who had been true to Him and who had called upon Him for protection. Daniel's praying was an essential factor in defeating the king's decree and in discomfiting the wicked, envious rulers, who had set the trap for Daniel in order to destroy him and remove him from place and power in the kingdom.

My Response

....

....

....

....

....

....

....

....

....

....

....

....

....

....

My Response

....

....

....

....

....

....

....

....

....

....

....

....

....

11
Our Sufficiency Is of God

But above all he excelled in prayer.
The inwardness and weight of his spirit, the
reverence and solemnity of his address and
behavior, and the fewness and fullness of his
words have often struck even strangers with
admiration as they used to reach others with
consolation. The most awful, living, reverend
frame I ever felt or beheld, I must say, was his
prayer. And truly it was a testimony. He knew
and lived nearer to the Lord than other men,
for they that know him most will see most reason
to approach him with reverence and fear.

WILLIAM PENN OF GEORGE FOX

The sweetest graces by a slight perversion may bear the bitterest fruit. The sun gives life, but sunstrokes are death. Preaching is to give life; it may kill. The preacher holds the keys; he

[Editor's note: This is another chapter that Bounds wrote specifically to preachers. As you read, insert the word witness for preacher or preaching, and see how the message of prayer applies to your everyday life.]

may lock as well as unlock. Preaching is God's great institution for the planting and maturing of spiritual life. When properly executed, its benefits are untold; when wrongly executed, no evil can exceed its damaging results. It is an easy matter to destroy the flock if the shepherd is unwary or the pasture is destroyed, easy to capture the citadel if the watchmen is asleep or the food and water is poisoned. Invested with such gracious prerogatives, exposed to so great evils, involving so many grave responsibilities, it would be a mockery of the shrewdness of the devil and an insult on his character and reputation if he did not bring his master influences to adulterate the preacher and the preaching. In the face of all this, the exclamatory question of Paul, "Who is sufficient for these things?" (2 Corinthians 2:16) is never out of order.

Paul says: "Our sufficiency is of God; who also hath made us able ministers of the new testament; not of the letter, but of the spirit: for the letter killeth, but the spirit giveth life" (2 Corinthians 3:5–6). The true ministry is God-touched, God-enabled, and God-made. The Spirit of God is on the preacher in anointing power, the fruit of the Spirit is in his heart, the Spirit of God has vitalized the man and the word; his preaching gives life, gives life as the spring gives life; gives life as the resurrection gives life; gives ardent life as the summer gives ardent life; gives fruitful life as the autumn gives fruitful life. The life-giving preacher is a man of God, whose heart is ever thirsty for God, whose soul is ever following hard after God, whose eye is single to God, and in whom by the power of God's Spirit the flesh and the world have been crucified and his ministry is like the generous flood of a life-giving river.

The preaching that kills is nonspiritual preaching. The ability of the preaching is not from God. Lower sources than God have given to it energy and life. The Spirit is not evident in the preacher nor his preaching. Many kinds of forces may be projected and stimulated by preaching that kills, but they are not spiritual forces. They may resemble spiritual forces, but are only the shadow, the counterfeit; life they may seem to have, but the life is beguiling. The preaching that kills is the letter: shapely and orderly it may be, but it is the letter still—

the dry, husky letter, the empty, bald shell. The letter may have the germ of life in it, but it has no breath of spring to evoke it; winter seeds they are, as hard as the winter's soil, as icy as the winter's air, no thawing nor germinating by them. This letter-preaching has the truth. But even divine truth has no life-giving energy alone; it must be energized by the Spirit, with all God's forces at its back. Truth unquickened by God's Spirit deadens as much as, or more than, error. It may be the truth without the Spirit; but without the Spirit its shade and touch are deadly, its truth error, its light darkness. The letter-preaching is not soothing, neither mellowed nor oiled by the Spirit. There may be tears, but tears cannot run God's machinery; tears may be but summer's breath on a snow-covered iceberg, nothing but surface slush. Feelings and earnestness there may be, but it is the emotion of the actor and the earnestness of the attorney. The preacher may feel from the kindling of his own sparks, be eloquent over his own analysis, earnest in delivering the product of his own brain; the professor may usurp the place and imitate the fire of the apostle; brains and nerves may serve the place and feign the work of God's Spirit, and by these forces the letter may glow and sparkle like an illuminated text, but the glow and sparkle will be as barren of life as the field sown with pearls. The death-dealing element lies behind the words, behind the sermon, behind the occasion, behind the manner, behind the action. The great hindrance is in the preacher himself. He has not in himself the mighty life-creating forces. There may be no discount on his orthodoxy, honesty, cleanness, or earnestness; but somehow the man, the inner man, in its secret places has never broken down and surrendered to God; his inner life is not a great highway for the transmission of God's message, God's power. Somehow self and not God rules in the holy of holiest. Somewhere, all unconscious to himself, some spiritual nonconductor has touched his inner being, and the divine current has been arrested. His inner being has never felt its thorough spiritual bankruptcy, its utter powerlessness; he has never learned to cry out with an indescribable cry of self-despair and self-helplessness till God's power and God's fire come in and fill, purify, empower. Self-esteem, self-ability in some pernicious shape has defamed and violated the temple, which should be held sacred for God. Life-giving preaching costs the preacher much—death to self, crucifixion to the world, the travail of his own soul. Only crucified preaching can give life. Crucified preaching can come only from a crucified man.

My Response

....

....

....

....

....

....

....

....

....

....

....

....

....

....

My Response

....

....

....

....

....

....

....

....

....

....

....

....

....

12
Putting God to Work

*For since the beginning of the world men have
not heard, nor perceived by the ear, neither hath
the eye seen, O God, beside thee, what he hath
prepared for him that waiteth for him.*

ISAIAH 64:4

The assertion voiced in the title given this
chapter is but another way of declaring that
God has of His own motion placed Himself
under the law of prayer, and has obligated
Himself to answer the prayers of men. He has
ordained prayer as a means whereby He will
do things through men as they pray, which He
would not otherwise do. Prayer is a specific
divine appointment, an ordinance of heaven,
whereby God purposes to carry out His gracious designs on earth and to execute and make
efficient the plan of salvation.

When we say that prayer puts God to work,
it is simply to say that man has it in his power

by prayer to move God to work in His own way among men, in which way He would not work if prayer was not made. Thus while prayer moves God to work, at the same time God puts prayer to work. As God has ordained prayer, and as prayer has no existence separate from men, but involves men, then logically prayer is the one force that puts God to work in earth's affairs through men and their prayers.

Let these fundamental truths concerning God and prayer be kept in mind in all references to prayer, and in all our reading of the incidents of prayer in the scriptures.

If prayer puts God to work on earth, then, by the same token, prayerlessness rules God out of the world's affairs and prevents Him from working. And if prayer moves God to work in this world's affairs, then prayerlessness excludes God from everything concerning men and leaves man on earth the mere creature of circumstances, at the mercy of blind fate or without help of any kind from God. It leaves man in this world with its tremendous responsibilities and its difficult problems, and with all of its sorrows, burdens, and afflictions, without any God at all. In reality the denial of prayer is a denial of God Himself, for God and prayer are so inseparable that they can never be divorced.

Prayer affects three different spheres of existence—the divine, the angelic and the human. It puts God to work, it puts angels to work, and it puts man to work. It lays its hands upon God, angels, and men. What a wonderful reach there is in prayer! It brings into play the forces of heaven and earth. God, angels, and men are subjects of this wonderful law of prayer, and all these have to do with the possibilities and the results of prayer. God has so far subjected Himself to prayer that by reason of His own appointment, He is induced to work among men in a way in which He does not work if men do not pray. Prayer lays hold upon God and influences Him to work. This is the meaning of prayer as it concerns God. This is the doctrine of prayer, or else there is nothing whatever in prayer.

Prayer puts God to work in all things prayed for. While man in his weakness and poverty waits, trusts, and prays, God undertakes the work. "For since the beginning of the world men have not heard, nor perceived by the ear, neither hath the eye seen, O God, beside thee, what he hath prepared for him that waiteth for him" (Isaiah 64:4).

Jesus Christ commits Himself to the force of prayer. "Whatsoever ye shall ask in my name," He says, "that will I do, that the Father may be glorified in the Son. If ye shall ask any thing in my name, I will do it" (John 14:13–14). And again: "If ye abide in me, and my words abide in you, ye shall ask what ye will, and it shall be done unto you" (John 15:7).

To no other energy is the promise of God committed as to that of prayer. Upon no other force are the purposes of God so dependent as this one of prayer. The Word of God expounds on the results and necessity of prayer. The work of God stays or advances as prayer puts forth its strength. Prophets and apostles have urged the utility, force, and necessity of prayer. "I have set watchmen upon thy walls, O Jerusalem, which shall never hold their peace day nor night: Ye that make mention of the LORD, keep not silence, and give him no rest, till he establish,

and till he make Jerusalem a praise in the earth"
(Isaiah 62:6–7).

Prayer, with its antecedents and attendants, is the one and only condition of the final triumph of the Gospel. It is the one and only condition that honors the Father and glorifies the Son. Little and poor praying has weakened Christ's power on earth, postponed the glorious results of His reign, and retired God from His sovereignty.

Prayer puts God's work in His hands, and keeps it there. It looks to Him constantly and depends on Him implicitly to further His own cause. Prayer is but faith resting in, acting with, and leaning on and obeying God. This is why God loves it so well, why He puts all power into its hands, and why He so highly esteems men of prayer.

Every movement for the advancement of the Gospel must be created by and inspired by prayer. In all these movements of God, prayer precedes and attends as an invariable and necessary condition.

In this relation, God makes prayer identical in force and power with Himself and says to those on earth who pray: "You are on the earth to carry on My cause. I am in heaven, the Lord of all, the Maker of all, the Holy One of all. Now whatever you need for My cause, ask Me and I will do it. Shape the future by your prayers, and all that you need for present supplies, command Me. I made heaven and earth, and all things in them. Ask largely. Open thy mouth wide, and I will fill it. It is My work which you are doing. It concerns My cause. Be prompt and full in praying. Do not abate your asking, and I will not wince nor abate in My giving." Everywhere in His Word God conditions His actions on prayer. Everywhere in His Word His actions and attitude are shaped by prayer. To quote all the scriptural passages that prove the immediate, direct, and personal relation of prayer to God, would be to transfer whole pages of scripture to this study. Man has personal relations with God. Prayer is the divinely appointed means by which man comes into direct connection with God. By His own ordinance God holds Himself bound to hear prayer. God bestows His great good on His children when they seek it along the avenue of prayer.

When Solomon closed his great prayer that he offered at the dedication of the temple, God appeared to him, approved him, and laid down the universal principles of His action. In 2 Chronicles 7:12–15 we read as follows:

> And the LORD appeared to Solomon by night, and said unto him, I have heard thy prayer, and have chosen this place to myself for an house of sacrifice. If I shut up heaven that there be no rain, or if I command the locusts to devour the land, or if I send pestilence among my people; if my people which are called by my name, shall humble themselves, and pray, and seek my face, and turn from their wicked ways; then will I hear from heaven, and will forgive their sin, and will heal their land. Now mine eyes shall be open, and mine ears attend unto the prayer that is made in this place.

In His purposes concerning the Jews in the Babylonian captivity (Jeremiah 29:10–13)

God asserts His unfailing principles:

*For thus saith the LORD, That after
seventy years be accomplished at
Babylon, I will visit you, and perform
my good word toward you, in causing
you to return to this place. For I know
the thoughts that I think toward you,
saith the LORD, thoughts of peace,
and not of evil, to give you an expected
end. Then shall ye call upon me, and ye
shall go and pray unto me, and I will
hearken unto you. And ye shall seek me,
and find me, when ye shall search
for me with all your heart.*

In Bible terminology prayer means calling upon God for things we desire, asking things of God. Thus we read: "Call unto me, and I will answer thee, and show thee great and mighty things, which thou knowest not" (Jeremiah 33:3). "Call upon me in the day of trouble: I will deliver thee" (Psalm 50:15). "Then shalt thou call, and the LORD shall answer; thou shalt cry, and he shall say, Here I am" (Isaiah 58:9).

Prayer is revealed as a direct application to God for some temporal or spiritual good. It is an appeal to God to intervene in life's affairs for the good of those for whom we pray. God is recognized as the source and fountain of all good, and prayer implies that all His good is held in His keeping for those who call upon Him in truth.

That prayer is an application to God, intercourse with God, and communion with God, comes out strongly and simply in the praying of Old Testament saints. Abraham's intercession for Sodom is a striking illustration of the nature of prayer, intercourse with God, and the intercessory side of prayer. The declared purpose of God to destroy Sodom confronted Abraham, and his soul within him was greatly moved because of his great interest in that fated city. His nephew and family resided there. That purpose of God must be changed. God's decree for the destruction of this evil city's inhabitants must be revoked.

It was no small undertaking that faced Abraham when he conceived the idea of beseeching God to spare Sodom. Abraham sets himself to change God's purpose and to save Sodom with the other cities of the plain. It was certainly a most difficult and delicate work for him to throw his influence with God in favor of those doomed cities to save them.

He bases his plea on the simple fact of the number of righteous men who could be found in Sodom, and appeals to the infinite righteousness of God not to destroy the righteous with the wicked. "That be far from thee. . .to slay the righteous with the wicked. . . . Shall not the Judge of all the earth do right?" (Genesis 18:25). With what deep self-abasement and reverence does Abraham enter upon his high and divine work! He stood before God in solemn awe and meditation, and then drew near to God and spoke. He advanced step-by-step in faith, in demand and urgency, and God granted every request that he made. It has been well said that "Abraham left off asking before God left off granting." It seems that Abraham had a kind of optimistic view of the piety of Sodom. He scarcely expected when he undertook this matter to have it end in failure. He was greatly in earnest, and had every encouragement to press his case. In his final request he surely thought that with Lot, his wife, his daughters, his sons, and his sons-in-law, he had his ten righteous persons for whose sake God would spare the city. But alas! The count failed when the final test came. There were not ten righteous people in that large population.

But this was true. If he did not save Sodom by his persistent praying, the purposes of God were stayed for a season, and possibly had not Abraham's goodness of heart overestimated the number of pious people in that devoted city, God might have saved it had he reduced his figures still further.

This is an example of Old Testament praying that discloses God's mode of working through prayer. It shows further how God is moved to work in answer to prayer in this world, even when it comes to changing His purposes concerning a sinful community. This praying of Abraham was no mere performance, no dull, lifeless ceremony, but an earnest plea, a strong advocacy, to secure a desired end, to have an influence, one person with another person.

How full of meaning is this series of remarkable intercessions made by Abraham! Here we have arguments designed to convince God, and pleas to persuade God to change His purpose. We see deep humility, but holy boldness as well, perseverance, and advances made based on victory in each petition. Here we have enlarged asking encouraged by enlarged answers. God stays and answers as long as Abraham stays and asks. To Abraham God is existent, approachable, and all-powerful, but at the same time He defers to men, acts favorably on their desires, and grants them favors asked for. Not to pray is a denial of God, a denial of His existence, a denial of His nature, and a denial of His purposes toward humankind.

God has specifically to do with prayer promises in their breadth, certainty, and limitations. Jesus Christ presses us into the presence of God with these prayer promises, not only by the assurance that God will answer, but that no other being but God can answer. He presses us to God because only in this way can we move God to take a hand in earth's affairs and persuade Him to intervene in our behalf.

"All things, whatsoever ye ask in prayer,

believing, ye shall receive," says Jesus, (Matthew 21:22) and this all-comprehensive condition not only presses us to pray for all things, everything great and small, but it leads us toward and confines us to God, for who but God can cover the limitless universal things and can assure us certainly of receiving the very thing for which we may ask in all the thesaurus of earthly and heavenly good?

It is Jesus Christ, the Son of God, who makes demands on us to pray, and it is He who puts Himself and all He has so fully in the answer. He puts Himself at our service and answers our demands when we pray.

And just as He puts Himself and the Father at our command in prayer, to come directly into our lives and to work for our good, so also does He engage to answer the demands of two or more believers who are in agreement. "If two of you shall agree on earth as touching any thing that they shall ask, it shall be done for them of my Father which is in heaven" (Matthew 18:19). None but God could put Himself in a covenant so binding as that, for God only could fulfill such a promise and could reach to its exacting and all-controlling demands. God only can answer for the promises.

God needs prayer, and man needs prayer, too. It is indispensable to God's work in this world, and is essential to getting God to work in earth's affairs. So God binds men to pray by the most solemn obligations. God commands men to pray, and so not to pray is plain disobedience to an imperative command of almighty God. Without prayer the graces, the salvation, and the good of God are not bestowed on men. Prayer is a high privilege, a royal prerogative, and many and eternal are the losses by failure to exercise it. Prayer is the great, universal force to advance God's cause, the reverence that hallows God's name, the ability to do God's will, and the establishment of God's kingdom in the hearts of the children of men. These, and their coincidents and agencies, are created and affected by prayer.

One of the constitutional enforcements of the Gospel is prayer. Without prayer, the Gospel can neither be preached effectively, advocated faithfully, experienced in the heart, nor be practiced in the life. And for the very simple reason that by leaving prayer out of the catalog of religious duties, we leave God out, and His work cannot progress without Him.

The movements that God purposed under Cyrus, king of Persia, prophesied about by Isaiah many years before Cyrus was born, were conditioned on prayer. God declares His purpose, power, independence, and defiance of obstacles by carrying out those purposes. His omnipotent and absolutely infinite power is set to encourage prayer. He has been ordering all events, directing all conditions, and creating all things that He might answer prayer, and then turns Himself over to His praying ones to be commanded. And then all the results and power He holds in His hands will be bestowed in lavish and unmeasured generosity to carry out prayers and to make prayer the mightiest energy in the world.

The passage in Isaiah 45 is too lengthy to be quoted in its entirety, but it is well worth reading. It closes with such strong words as these, words about prayer, which are the climax of all that God has been saying concerning His purposes in connection with Cyrus:

"Thus saith the LORD, the Holy One of Israel, and his Maker, Ask me of things to come concerning my sons, and concerning the work of my hands command ye me. I have made the earth, and created man upon it: I, even my hands, have stretched out the heavens, and all their host have I commanded" (Isaiah 45:11–12).

In the conclusion of the history of Job, we see how God intervenes on behalf of Job and calls upon his friends to present themselves before Job that he may pray for them. "My wrath is kindled against thee, and against thy two friends" (Job 42:7), is God's statement, with the further words added, "My servant Job shall pray for you: for him will I accept" (Job 42:8), a striking illustration of God intervening to deliver Job's friends in answer to Job's prayer.

We have spoken of prayer affecting God, angels, and men. Christ wrote nothing while living. Memoranda, notes, sermon writing, sermon making were alien to Him. Autobiography was not to His taste. The revelation of John was His last utterance. In that book we have pictured the great importance, the priceless value, and the high position that prayer obtains in the movements, history, and unfolding progress of God's Church in this world. We have this picture in Revelation 8:3–5, disclosing the interest the angels in heaven have in the prayers of the saints and in accomplishing the answers to those prayers:

And another angel came and stood at the altar, having a golden censer; and there was given unto him much incense, that he should offer it with the prayers of all saints, upon the golden altar which was before the throne. And the smoke of the incense, which came with the prayers of the saints, ascended up before God out of the angel's hand. And the angel took the censer, and filled it with fire of the altar, and cast it into the earth: and there were voices, and thunderings, and lightnings, and an earthquake.

Translated into the prose of everyday life, these words show how the capital stock by which heaven carries on the business of salvation under Christ, is made up of the prayers of God's saints on earth, and discloses how these prayers in flaming power come back to earth and produce its mighty commotions, influences, and revolutions.

Praying men are essential to almighty God in all His plans and purposes. God's secrets, councils, and cause have never been committed to prayerless men. Neglect of prayer has always brought loss of faith, loss of love, and loss of prayer. Failure to pray has been the baneful, inevitable cause of backsliding and estrangement from God. Prayerless men have stood in the way of God fulfilling His Word and doing His will on earth. They tie the divine hands and interfere with God in His gracious designs. As praying men are a help to God, so prayerless men are a hindrance to Him.

We press the scriptural view of the necessity of prayer, even at the cost of repetition. The subject is too important for repetition to weaken or tire, too vital to be trite or tame. We must feel it anew. The fires of prayer have burned low. Ashes and not flames are on its altars.

No insistence in the scriptures is more pressing than prayer. No exhortation is more often reiterated, none is more hearty, none is more solemn and stirring, than to pray. No principle is more strongly and broadly declared than that which urges us to prayer. There is no duty to which we are more strongly obliged than the obligation to pray. There is no command more imperative and insistent than that of praying. Art thou praying in everything without ceasing, in the closet, hidden from the eyes of men, and praying always and everywhere? That is the personal, pertinent, and all-important question for every soul.

Many instances occur in God's Word showing that God intervenes in this world in answer to prayer. Nothing is clearer when the Bible is consulted than that almighty God is brought directly into the things of this world by the praying of His people. Jonah flees from duty and takes ship for a distant port. But God follows him, and by a strange providence this disobedient prophet is cast out of the vessel, and the God who sent him to Nineveh prepares a fish to swallow him. In the fish's belly he cries out to the God against whom he had sinned, and God intervenes and causes the fish to vomit Jonah out on dry land. Even the fishes of the great deep are subject to the law of prayer.

Likewise the birds of the air are brought into subjection to this same law. Elijah had foretold to Ahab the coming of that prolonged drought, and food and even water became scarce. God sent him to the brook Cherith, and said unto him, "It shall be, that thou shalt drink of the brook; and I have commanded the ravens to feed thee there. . . . And the ravens brought him bread and flesh in the morning, and bread and flesh in the evening" (1 Kings 17:4, 6). Can anyone doubt that this man of God, who later on shut up and opened the rain clouds by prayer was not praying about this time, when so much was at stake? God interposed among the birds of the air this time and strangely moved them to take care of His servant so that he would not want food and water.

David in an evil hour, instead of listening to the advice of Joab, his prime minister, yielded to the suggestion of Satan and counted the people, which displeased God. So God told him to choose one of three evils as a retribution for his folly and sin. Pestilence came among the people in violent form, and David prayed.

"And David said unto God, Is it not I that commanded the people to be numbered? even I it is that hath sinned and done evil indeed; but as for these sheep, what have they done? let thine hand, I pray thee, O LORD my God, be on me, and on my father's house; but not on thy people, that they should be plagued" (1 Chronicles 21:17).

And though God had been greatly grieved at David for numbering Israel, He could not resist this appeal of a penitent and prayerful spirit, and God was moved by prayer to put His hand on the springs of disease and stop the fearful plague. God was put to work by David's prayer.

Numbers of other cases could be named. These are sufficient. God seems to have taken great pains in His divine revelation to men to show how He interferes in earth's affairs in answer to the praying of His saints.

The question might arise here in some overcritical minds who are not strong believers in prayer as to the so-called laws of nature, as if there was a conflict between what they call the laws of nature and the law of prayer. These people make nature a sort of imaginary god entirely separate of almighty God. What is nature anyway? It is but the creation of God, the Maker of all things. And what are the laws of nature but the laws of God, through which He governs the material world. As the law of prayer is also the law of God, there cannot possibly be any conflict between the two sets of laws, but all must work in perfect harmony. Prayer does not violate any natural law. God may set aside one law for the higher working of another law, and this He may do when He answers prayer. Or almighty God may answer prayer working through the course of natural law. But whether or not we understand it, God is over and above all nature, and can and will answer prayer in a wise, intelligent, and just manner, even though man may not comprehend it. So that in no sense is there any discord or conflict between God's several laws when God is persuaded to interfere with human affairs in answer to prayer.

In this connection another word might be said. We used the form of words to which there can be no objection, that prayer does certain things, but this of course implies not that prayer as a human means accomplishes anything, but that prayer only accomplishes things instrumentally. Prayer is the instrument; God is the efficient and active agent. So that prayer in itself does not interfere in earth's affairs, but prayer in the hands of men moves God to intervene and do things, which He would not otherwise do if prayer was not used as the instrument.

It is as we say, "faith hath saved thee" (Luke 7:50), by which is simply meant that God through the faith of the sinner saves him, faith being only the instrument used by the sinner that brings salvation to him.

My Response

....

....

....

....

....

....

....

....

....

....

....

....

....

....

My Response

....

....

....

....

....

....

....

....

....

....

....

....

....

My Response

....

....

....

....

....

....

....

....

....

....

....

....

....